THE NAVAL WAR IN THE WEST
WEST
The Wolf Packs

The Illustrated History of World War II

THE NAVAL WAR
IN THE WEST
The Wolf Packs

by Trevor Nevitt Dupuy

FRANKLIN WATTS

London   ·   New York

Franklin Watts Limited
18, Grosvenor Street
London, W.1

First published in Great Britain 1965

Original edition published in the United States of America by
FRANKLIN WATTS, INC.

Copyright © 1963 by Franklin Watts, Inc.

SBN 85166 024 X

ACKNOWLEDGMENTS OF PHOTOGRAPHS

Pages 2, 40, 59: PHOTO FROM EUROPEAN
Pages 4, 31, 51: PHOTO FROM THREE LIONS
Pages 5, 30: NAVY DEPARTMENT PHOTOS NO. 80-G-68693 AND NO. 80-G-74822 IN
    THE (U.S.) NATIONAL ARCHIVES
Pages 8, 11, 12, 14, 19, 21, 25, 43, 47, 49, 52: THE IMPERIAL WAR MUSEUM, LONDON
Page 23: PHOTO FROM PIX INCORPORATED
Pages 28, 33, 36: PHOTO FROM WIDE WORLD
Page 38: PHOTO FROM E. C. ARMÉES, FRANCE
Page 54: USIA PHOTO NO. 306-NT-1290-5 IN THE (U.S.) NATIONAL ARCHIVES

Printed Offset in Great Britain by
STRAKER BROTHERS LTD
Bishopsgate, London, E.C.2

TO KIM

Contents

THE NAVAL WAR IN THE WEST
WEST
The Wolf Packs

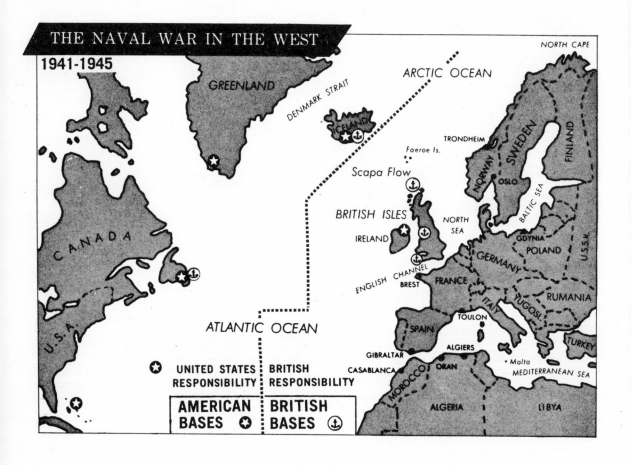

THE NAVAL WAR IN THE WEST

1941-1945

The Battle of the Atlantic

The Early Days of the Battle

'THE BATTLE OF THE ATLANTIC', as Winston Churchill was the first to call it, was fought between the German submarine fleet and the Allied navies for control of the Atlantic sea-lanes leading to the British Isles. This fierce, relentless struggle actually began on 3 September, 1939, the very first day of World War II, but it did not reach its peak until ten months later.

When World War II began, the Germans had less than sixty submarines. Of these, only twenty or thirty were available to prowl the oceans at any one time. The other submarines were either on their way out to the Atlantic sea-lanes, or returning from them, or on training missions, or being resupplied or repaired in port. But German shipyards were not idle. By the middle of 1940 the intensive German construction programme had produced many more U-boats.

What was still more important to the outcome of this ruthless battle was the fact that Hitler's conquest of Norway and France had given Germany a number of new seaports that could be used as submarine bases. These ports were much closer to the sea-lanes than were those under the control of Germany when the war started. This meant that German U-boats could go out on patrol and return more quickly. This gave them more time actually to lurk in the sea-lanes, where they could attack British and Allied merchant shipping.

1

Mass production of submarines in German shipyards

The Wolf Packs

FOLLOWING HIS VICTORY over France, Hitler had hoped that Britain would make peace with Germany. When Churchill refused to consider German peace offers in June 1940, Hitler ordered his strengthened U-boat fleet to make an all-out attack on British shipping.

The commander of the German undersea fleet was Karl Doenitz, who had himself commanded a German U-boat during World War I. Doenitz had carefully studied the lessons of that war, and knew that German submarines had almost—but not quite—knocked Britain out of the war by cutting off food and other supplies to the British Isles. Britain had managed to survive only by starting the convoy system in 1917.

Doenitz believed that he could overcome the British convoy system with the bigger, faster, more powerful submarines at his command in World War II. He had worked out a plan that would make the best use of them with a system of what he called the 'wolf packs'. From his headquarters at the French port of Lorient, Doenitz was able to control wolf-pack operations personally.

A German wolf pack consisted of fifteen or twenty U-boats. These submarines spread out over the likely sea-lanes west of the British Isles, and then waited for British convoys to pass by. While waiting, they sometimes sighted individual ships, which they attacked if they could. But if one of the U-boats sighted a convoy, it did not attack right away. Instead, it reported by radio directly to Doenitz, telling him the location, size, direction and speed of the convoy. Then the lone submarine followed the convoy, avoiding the cruiser and destroyer escorts, but always keeping its prey in sight.

*German U-boats put in
at Kiel for refuelling*

Back at his headquarters in Lorient, Doenitz then radioed orders to the other members of the wolf pack to close in for an attack. When enough submarines were assembled near the convoy— usually on the first night after it was sighted—the pack attacked. As soon as the U-boats had fired their torpedoes, they dived below the surface to escape the powerful, explosive depth charges fired by the warships that escorted the convoy. As soon as the escort ships gave up the chase, the submarines returned to follow the convoy and attack again. Night after night they repeated this pattern of attack—running away, and then returning to attack again and again until the surviving ships of the convoy finally reached port.

Britain put on escort duty every available destroyer or other small, fast warship, as well as a number of armed merchant cruisers, but there simply were not enough of them to protect the convoys. The British warships sank an average of three or four U-boats a month, but the German shipyards were turning out new ones faster than the old ones could be destroyed. On the other side, the U-boats were sinking an average of three or four British merchant ships every day—at more than six times the rate of new construction in the British Isles. In the year between June 1940 and June 1941, the Germans sank more than 1,300 British

An Allied escort carrier plane drops explosives on a surfaced German submarine

merchant ships. In actual weight, based on the amount of cargo the various ships could carry, this meant that the U-boats destroyed about 5,700,000 tons of British shipping. In that same year, the British were able to build barely 800,000 tons.

The British Strike Back

BEFORE THE END of 1940, the British had added long-range air escort to their convoys, using aircraft based in northern Scotland, northern Ireland, Iceland and Canada. The presence of these planes made the U-boats more cautious, but it did not seriously interfere with the success of their operations, because the British planes could patrol only over a few hundred miles from shore. The wolf packs simply moved out of reach to the middle of the Atlantic and continued their deadly attacks.

In the crowded sea-lanes south-west of Britain, long-range German Focke-Wulf bombers, based in France, also joined the attack against British shipping. There was little the British could do against these big bombers, for the British fighter planes simply did not have enough range to interfere with them, and there were no aircraft carriers available. On 6 March 1941, the Prime Minister, Winston Churchill, issued an order to the fighting services:

'We must take the offensive against the U-boat and the Focke-Wulf wherever we can and whenever we can. The U-boat at sea must be hunted, the U-boat in the building yard or in dock must be bombed. The Focke-Wulf and other bombers employed against our shipping must be attacked in the air and in their nests.'

In the month following Churchill's directive, the Royal Navy and the Royal Air Force redoubled their efforts to protect the convoys. They sank several U-boats, including the one commanded by the skilful submarine commander, Gunther Prien, who had sunk the big British battleship *Royal Oak* inside the anchorage at Scapa Flow in 1939.

The British also stepped up their air raids against the German U-boat bases in France and Germany, but the Germans countered by building great submarine 'pens', putting roofs of reinforced concrete, several feet thick, over the submarine docks. The British bombs burst harmlessly on these concrete roofs.

In April 1941, in an attempt to make up for the desperate shortage of aircraft carriers, four Royal Naval 'fighter catapult ships' joined the convoy escorts. These were followed by the 'catapult-aircraft merchant ships', or CAM-ships, which, like the fighter catapult ships, each carried one fighter on a catapult— but were different from the former in that the aircraft was operated by the special Merchant Service Fighter Unit of the Royal Air Force, and the ship was a merchantman carrying normal cargo. After an attack, a pilot had to face ditching or bailing out into the sea.

The catapult ships did useful work, but much more effective were the small escort carriers. The first of these was HMS *Audacity*, a captured German merchant ship cut down to accommodate a flight deck. She escorted her first convoy in September 1941 and was a great success. The *Audacity* had no hangar and carried only six or eight Martlet fighters, but her little squadron drove off Focke-Wulfs and helped the other escorts to sink several U-boats before she was sunk in December, after the surprised Germans had made a concentrated attack on her. More merchantman-into-

A Hurricane fighter being catapulted from a CAM-ship.
Below: *HMS* Audacity

carrier conversions were planned as a result of her success, but meanwhile British merchant-ship sinkings continued at an alarming rate.

Neutral America Joins the Battle of the Atlantic

IN AUGUST 1941, there had been a momentous conference between the British Prime Minister Winston Churchill and the American President Roosevelt in Placentia Bay, Newfoundland. Churchill had sailed across the Atlantic in the battleship HMS *Repulse*. Roosevelt had arrived in the cruiser USS *Augusta*. On the decks of their warships, the two leaders had agreed on the famous Atlantic Charter, which pledged their countries to preserve freedom and to improve world conditions after the war. They had also discussed Britain's terrible losses in the Battle of the Atlantic.

Although the United States was not then at war with Germany, Roosevelt had recognized the fact that all countries of the western world would be in grave danger if Hitler starved Britain into surrender. Furthermore, the American president had felt that the appearance of German submarines in the waters of the Western Hemisphere was a direct threat to the United States. So he had informed Churchill that the American navy would not permit German submarines to attack British shipping in any part of the Atlantic Ocean west of Iceland.

Roosevelt's decision was announced to the world on 14 August. Immediately afterwards the U.S. Navy began to escort all British convoys in the western part of the North Atlantic. This freed British warships for escort duty in the eastern part of the ocean, where German attacks were growing ever more destructive.

9

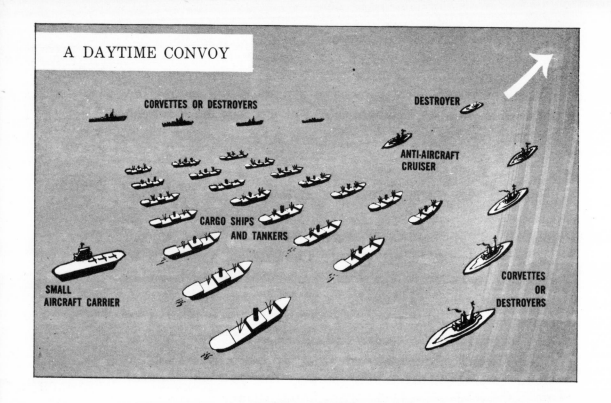

A DAYTIME CONVOY

CORVETTES OR DESTROYERS

DESTROYER

ANTI-AIRCRAFT
CRUISER

CARGO SHIPS
AND TANKERS

CORVETTES
OR
DESTROYERS

SMALL
AIRCRAFT CARRIER

In October the Germans began to attack convoys escorted by American ships in the western Atlantic. They sank a number of British merchantmen. On 16 October, a German submarine torpedoed the American destroyer USS *Kearny*. The *Kearny* managed to limp to Iceland for emergency repairs. On 31 October, the Germans torpedoed and sank the destroyer USS *Reuben James* about 600 miles west of Iceland. Although the United States was still technically at peace with Germany, the American navy found itself fighting vigorously on the side of Germany's adversary in the Battle of the Atlantic.

As the month of December 1941 began, the outlook for Britain was still very grim. Despite the fact that British shipyards had turned out many more vessels than they had done in 1940, and although American shipyards were producing still more vessels to help in the Battle of the Atlantic and carry food and other supplies to Britain, the scales still weighed heavily in favour of the Germans. Their U-boats were sinking more than twice as many ships as the combined efforts of Britain and the United States could produce.

Then suddenly, on 7 December, the Japanese attacked the American naval base at Pearl Harbour in the Pacific Ocean. Four days later, Germany rallied to the side of her Axis partner and declared war on the United States. Immediately Doenitz sent several of his wolf packs to roam the coastal waters of America. The United States was now Britain's official partner in the desperate Battle of the Atlantic.

A small British Hunt-class destroyer attacks an enemy submarine with depth charges

A British cruiser in heavy winter seas during a convoy run to Murmansk

The Murmansk Convoys

Help for Russia

In June 1941, Hitler sent his armies into Soviet Russia. The Germans won spectacular victories as they drove closer and closer to the Soviet capital of Moscow. But fortunately for the Allies, Hitler personally interfered with the way his generals were running the war in Russia, and he made some serious mistakes. As a result, the Russian armies rallied just outside Moscow. By this time winter had begun, and it was a particularly severe one, even for northern Russia. Temperatures fell to as little as 60 degrees below zero. Totally unprepared for such weather, the Germans staggered back as the Russians counter-attacked. By the end of 1941, the land war in Russia had settled into a stalemate.

Both Russia and her Western allies—Britain and America—knew that the Germans would renew their attacks in Russia during the spring and summer of 1942. In the battles of 1941 the Russians had lost most of their guns, trucks and tanks. Many of their factories producing for the war industry had been overrun by the German armies. It was very doubtful whether the Russians could stop the Germans again in the spring unless Britain and America provided them with equipment to replace what they had lost. Britain immediately began to ship supplies to Russia.

There was only one ice-free Russian seaport that could be reached by British ships in winter as well as in summer. This was Murmansk, on the northern, Arctic Ocean, coast of Russia. In the summer-time the British ships could also use the nearby port of Archangel. In order to reach either Archangel or Murmansk, the supply convoys had to steam past the German-held coast of Norway.

The British began their convoys to north Russia in August 1941. In the summer months the British convoys steamed north of Bear Island. But at that time of the year, the northern days are practically endless. Darkness never really comes. German long-range bombers and surface ships had no trouble in finding and attacking the convoys. And while the bombing planes rained their explosives from the air, the U-boats, too, struck at the merchant ships and their hardworking escorts.

When winter came, the violent storms and almost constant darkness of the northern latitudes often prevented the German

German planes launch an attack on an Allied convoy carrying supplies to Murmansk. In the foreground is a Tribal-*class destroyer*

bombers from finding the British merchant ships. The U-boats, however, were still able to take a high toll of the convoys. This was because the Arctic ice pack closed in south of Bear Island, so that the British convoys could not get very far north of the Norwegian coast. Using their familiar wolf-pack tactics, the German submarines quickly found the convoys, and then kept up their attacks through the long Arctic nights.

Winter and summer, therefore, the Murmansk convoys presented a continual nightmare to the British merchant sailors and to the Royal Navy's escort ships. Losses were even heavier than on the North Atlantic sea-lanes. But Russia's need was so great that the British felt they must continue to send supplies. The Allies were afraid that they might never be able to defeat Hitler and his Nazis if Russia was knocked out of the war before America was ready to fight. The British gritted their teeth and continued to send their convoys to Murmansk.

The Ordeal of PQ-17

BY EARLY 1942 the Germans had begun to concentrate powerful air, surface and submarine forces in Norway, for the purpose of causing as much damage as possible to the convoys. The Admiralty in Britain was particularly disturbed to discover that the giant German battleship *Tirpitz* had arrived in Trondheim Fjord. This great warship was even more heavily armoured than her sister ship, the *Bismarck*. Joining her in Norwegian waters were the pocket battleships *Scheer* and *Lutzow*, and the heavy cruisers *Hipper* and *Prinz Eugen*.

15

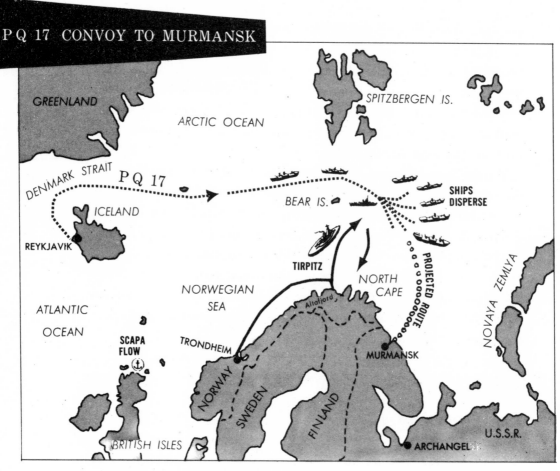

GREENLAND

ARCTIC OCEAN

SPITZBERGEN IS.

DENMARK STRAIT

P Q 17

BEAR IS.

SHIPS DISPERSE

ICELAND

REYKJAVIK

TIRPITZ

NORTH CAPE

PROJECTED ROUTE

NOVAYA ZEMLYA

ATLANTIC OCEAN

NORWEGIAN SEA

Altafjord

SCAPA FLOW

TRONDHEIM

MURMANSK

NORWAY

SWEDEN

FINLAND

U.S.S.R.

BRITISH ISLES

ARCHANGEL

British bombers and torpedo planes tried time after time to attack the *Tirpitz* in Trondheim Fjord, but they were unable to hit the great ship. In March, twelve torpedo planes from the aircraft carrier HMS *Victorious* attacked the *Tirpitz* as she was on her way north to Narvik, but all the torpedoes missed their target. The German battleship seemed to have a charmed life.

Between March and early June of 1942, British convoys PQ-12, PQ-13, PQ-14, PQ-15 and PQ-16 had all sailed from Scotland or

16

Iceland to Murmansk. (The letters 'PQ' were used to designate the British convoys to Murmansk). All five of the convoys had suffered heavy losses, in which several British cruisers and destroyers were included. Then, on 27 June, a convoy of thirty-four merchant ships left Iceland for the Russian port. This was PQ-17, escorted by four cruisers, two anti-aircraft cruisers, nine destroyers and seventeen smaller escort vessels. At the same time, an Allied covering force of two battleships, one aircraft carrier, three cruisers and eight destroyers was in the North Sea, ready to strike if the German battleships came out.

On 4 July, swarms of German aircraft began a series of attacks against convoy PQ-17. They succeeded in sinking three merchant ships. That same day the Admiralty learned that a German squadron consisting of the battleship *Tirpitz,* the two pocket battleships, the cruiser *Hipper* and several German destroyers had gone to sea. The reports showed that the German ships would be able to reach the British convoy long before the Allied covering force could catch up with them. The British rightly feared that the German ships, supported by *Luftwaffe* planes, would over-whelm the escort vessels and then sink all the merchant ships.

In an effort to deceive the Germans, the British escort cruisers sailed westwards, hoping to draw the German warships after them. At the same time the merchant ships were ordered to scatter and each to head by herself for Murmansk.

In fact, the German surface ships were moving very cautiously, and were not so close to the convoy as the Admiralty had feared. With most of these escort vessels gone, and with the merchant ships scattered over the face of the ocean, German submarines and bomber planes had a field day. They sank twenty more of the British merchant ships. Out of the thirty-four ships that had started in the convoy, only eleven finally straggled in to Murmansk.

To make matters worse, the Russians refused to believe that twenty-three ships of the convoy had been sunk. They accused the Western Allies of inventing a story of great losses, and of pretending to be giving more help than they really were doing. The suspicious Russians never understood the terrible conditions that the convoys encountered in sailing to Murmansk. They had no idea of the tremendous losses suffered by the crews of the escort vessels and by the merchant seamen bringing help to Russia. Yet without those supplies that did arrive, through Murmansk and through the Persian Gulf, Russia would probably have been defeated by the German armies in the summer of 1942.

After the disaster to PQ-17, the Allies were temporarily forced to discontinue their convoys to Murmansk. The Battle of the Atlantic was at its peak, and there were not enough warships to protect convoys on both the North Atlantic and the Arctic oceans. The Admiralty realized, too, that convoy losses on the Murmansk run were less during the dark and stormy winter days than during the summer when twenty-four hours of daylight made it easy for the expert German bombers to hit their targets. When the convoys started again, later in the year, there were enough Allied escort ships available to give them better protection.

Climax in the Mediterranean

The Importance of Malta

FROM THE OUTSET of the war in the Mediterranean, both sides had recognized the importance of Malta as a vital link in the British line of communications from Gibraltar to Alexandria and the Suez Canal. But its importance became even greater late in 1940, when Hitler decided to send Rommel and the *Afrika Korps* to help the Italians in North Africa.

Fighters and torpedo bombers ranged on the deck of a British aircraft carrier escorting a Malta convoy

German and Italian troop convoys and supply ships had to cross the central Mediterranean close to Malta. British aircraft, submarines and surface ships based on Malta could inflict serious damage on Axis vessels trying to maintain Rommel's line of communications. Four British destroyers, under Captain Mack in the *Jervis*, patrolling east of Malta on the night of 15-16 April, 1941, forcibly proved this to the Germans and Italians.

The moon was shining brightly, and the British lookouts saw several darkened ships sailing southwards towards the coast of Libya. It was a convoy of five Axis merchant ships, loaded with supplies, escorted by three Italian destroyers. The British squadron attacked immediately and sank all eight of the Axis ships, losing only one of their own.

Because of such losses, the Axis leaders decided that they must destroy the British base at Malta. German and Italian planes, from bases in Sicily and Italy, increased their attacks on the island, but Malta was rightly known as an 'unsinkable aircraft carrier'. Although Axis planes and ships took their toll of British convoys bringing in supplies and reinforcements, the British on Malta inflicted far more punishment than they received. By the autumn of 1941, the flow of supplies to Rommel had been cut down to a trickle.

Disaster Strikes the British Fleet

HITLER NOW REALIZED that he would have to use much stronger forces if he expected to smash Malta and gain control over the Mediterranean sea routes, and so he ordered more German submarines and *Luftwaffe* units to the Mediterranean. In November, one of the submarines sank the British carrier HMS *Ark Royal*

Italian aircraft try to sink the British aircraft carrier Ark Royal *in the Mediterranean*

as she was escorting a convoy. Britain had no other carriers that could be sent to the Mediterranean to replace her.

Then, on 25 December, the German submarine *U-331* torpedoed and sank the battleship HMS *Barham*, with heavy loss of British life. A few days later, the cruiser HMS *Galatea* went down, another victim of the intensified U-boat offensive in the Mediterranean. But the greatest blow of all had been struck at the Allies a few days earlier, on 19 December, through one of the few really heroic Italian naval exploits of the war.

That night three 'human torpedoes'—in fact, Italian midget submarines carrying two men each—had secretly entered Alexandria harbour. Using strong magnets, the courageous men in the tiny submarines had attached powerful time-fused explosive charges to the hulls of the only battleships remaining to the British Mediterranean fleet: HMS *Queen Elizabeth* and HMS *Valiant*. Both ships had been seriously damaged by the explosions, and were out of action for many months. The Italians had escaped.

As if this were not enough, that very day three British cruisers and a destroyer had run into a minefield, laid probably by a German U-boat. The destroyer and one of the cruisers had been sunk; the other two vessels had been gravely damaged, and were out of action for several months. If the Italian fleet had made a major effort, it might have swept the remnants of British sea power from the Mediterranean. As it was, the commander of the British Mediterranean fleet, Sir Andrew Cunningham, bluffed the Italians by boldly sending the few remaining British cruisers and destroyers out to sea. The bluff worked: although the Italians had many more ships and planes than the British, they were too timid to take advantage of their opportunity.

But no matter how bold or how efficient they were, the over-worked vessels of Cunningham's tiny fleet were unable to interfere effectively with the increasing number of Axis convoys supplying Rommel's army in Libya.

The German Air Offensive Against Malta

IN DECEMBER 1941, the German Commander Albert Kesselring took control in Italy. He had orders from Hitler to gain complete

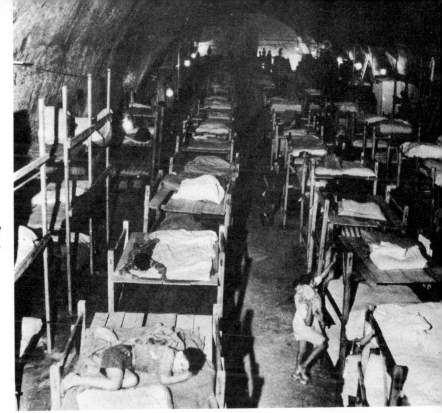

Air-raid shelters, dug deep into the rock in Malta, helped the island to survive over a thousand attacks from Axis planes

dominance over the air and the sea between Italy and North Africa, as well as to destroy the British base of Malta. In addition to the air units already attacking the island, Kesselring was given the Second German Air Fleet, consisting of 500 planes, to be stationed in Sicily.

Despite stormy weather, the Germans and Italians stepped up their air attacks on Malta in both numbers and intensity. In March 1942, they staged more than 300 raids—an average of ten or more each day. The only reason that the outnumbered British planes were able to keep up any sort of a fight against this massive air attack was that the Royal Navy stubbornly continued to deliver reinforcements, fuel, ammunition and other needed supplies to

Malta. But as the Germans increased their air superiority over the island and its surrounding waters, the problem of supplying the British base became a more and more difficult one. By early 1942, the British were being forced to protect each single supply ship with several of their scarce cruisers and destroyers. Although losses in ships and supplies were staggering, Churchill and his military advisers believed that to keep the Malta base in existence was worth what it cost.

In addition to their constant fight against air attacks, the British convoy escorts had several sharp engagements with strong Italian naval forces. In one of these engagements, the Battle of Sirte, in March 1942, a force of only four light cruisers and four destroyers, under Philip Vian, drove off an Italian squadron of one battleship, three cruisers and six destroyers.

By April, the British were finally forced to withdraw their few surviving surface ships from Malta and station them at the British bases at Gibraltar and Alexandria. In May, the British removed their submarines from the island. But the Royal Air Force continued to send in Spitfire fighters to challenge German air superiority over the central Mediterranean. British carriers brought these planes past the powerful fortress of Gibraltar into the western Mediterranean Sea. Then the planes flew off to Malta, before the carriers came too dangerously close to the Axis air bases. In April and May, the American carrier USS *Wasp* brought in 120 British fighters to join this bitter, never-ending battle over the tiny island.

These British planes, however, were so much outnumbered, and kept so busy defending the island against Axis attacks, that they could do little to interfere with the supply convoys to Rommel in North Africa. In May, Kesselring informed Hitler that he had completely neutralized the British base at Malta.

A British light cruiser throws out a smoke screen to shield a Malta convoy as another British cruiser elevates her forward 5·25 guns ready to shell the Italian fleet.

Below: Hurricane fighters on a Maltese airfield, with a pilot returning from a fight

Supply Convoys: Axis and Allied Victories

WITH HIS SUPPLY LINE more secure, Rommel had been able to start a new Axis land offensive in North Africa. In January 1942, he had driven the British back almost to Tobruk. Then, in May, as more supplies and reinforcements reached him, he attacked again. He won a great victory at Bir Hacheim, captured Tobruk and drove the British army back to El Alamein—only sixty miles from Alexandria. There he waited for more supplies to reach him, so that he could sweep the British completely from North Africa.

Kesslering, however, had been too optimistic about 'neutralizing Malta'. Even though the Germans continued to hammer the island throughout the summer of 1942, and even though the British continued to take terrible losses in merchant shipping and the escorting warships, some supplies got through to the British base. The Royal Navy was now using battleships and carriers to protect the convoys. Both British and American carriers continued to deliver planes to within flying distance of the beleaguered island. Some of these planes were new, longer-range torpedo craft, and they set out immediately to attack the Axis supply ships supporting Rommel. By September, British planes from Malta, working closely with submarines based in Alexandria and on Gibraltar, were sinking more than a third of the flow of supplies that Rommel needed so desperately in his battle positions in Egypt.

In November, British tenacity paid off. British planes and submarines sank more than three-quarters of the ships carrying supplies and reinforcements to Rommel. What the German general might have done if he had received these shipments, we do not know. Without them, he lost the Battle of El Alamein to the British, commanded by Bernard L. Montgomery. The victorious

26

British chased the Germans all the way across Egypt and Libya. Rommel's retreat was orderly and very fast, but Montgomery managed to keep up with him, because the British Mediterranean fleet was able to deliver supplies to the British army through captured Libyan seaports.

The Battle of El Alamein was the beginning of the end for the Axis in North Africa. Montgomery and his Eighth Army deserve great credit for their victory, but victory would have been impossible had not the Royal Navy been able to bring planes and supplies to Malta, and the Royal Air Force able to protect the the island and to destroy Axis convoys to North Africa.

Final Operations in the Mediterranean

IN EARLY NOVEMBER, even before Montgomery had begun his attack against Rommel at El Alamein, combined British and American land and sea forces had begun the amphibious invasion of French Morocco and Algeria. A powerful American naval squadron, under the then Rear Admiral H. Kent Hewitt, had protected the convoy of American troopships that brought Patton and his men from the United States to Morocco. Smaller British naval task forces had escorted British and American troops from England to landing beaches near Oran and Algiers. Additional protection for these two convoys had been provided by Force H under James Somerville—four battleships, two carriers, four cruisers and seventeen destroyers. These had cruised the Mediterranean west of Sardinia and Sicily, in order to prevent an attack by the Italian fleet.

The Italians had not come out, and the Allied troops, after two

American troops crowd the deck of a transport nearing North Africa

days of sharp fighting with Vichy troops, had secured Algeria and Morocco. Once the Frenchmen had surrendered, most of them joined the Free French army of General Charles de Gaulle.

Although Rommel had been defeated at El Alamein in November, a hard winter of land fighting in Tunisia lay ahead for the Allies. The German general had reorganized his troops even as they retreated, and in February, during the Battle of Kasserine Pass, was able to push forward again to within twenty miles of Tebessa, in eastern Algeria, where the main supply and communications centre of the Allied armies was located. But the day of great German victories in Africa was coming to an end. Rommel's troops received their supplies across the narrow Sicilian channel between Tunisia and Sicily. Fast German supply ships could make the trip easily in one night, but now most of them were caught by the alert Allied destroyers, motor torpedo boats and submarines of Cunningham's fleet. When in May 1943 the Germans and Italians in Tunisia were finally defeated, none of them were able to escape. The Allied fleet had them completely blockaded. A quarter of a million prisoners were taken by Allied soldiers.

After Tunisia, the next target for the Allies was Sicily. In July, two great invasion fleets sailed from North Africa past the indomitable little island of Malta, from which R.A.F. planes took off to provide air cover. The westernmost of these fleets was American, under Hewitt, recently promoted to vice admiral. To the east, the British armada was commanded by then Vice Admiral Sir Bertram H. Ramsay. Again the battleships and cruisers of Force H were close by, in company with two powerful cruiser squadrons, to make sure that the Italians did not interfere. And again the Italian navy did not choose to fight.

In a little over a month, Montgomery's and Patton's British and

The USS Boise *bombards the coast of Sicily*

American soldiers conquered Sicily. Then the Allied armies and navies prepared to invade Italy itself. But the Italians were ready to leave the war. On 9 September, the very day the Allied troops went ashore at Salerno, Italy surrendered to the Allies. Under Allied orders, the Italian fleet immediately sailed out in order to prevent its being taken over by the Germans. German aeroplanes attacked the Italian warships as they steamed south to Malta, sinking one battleship and damaging several other vessels; but most of the Italian ships got through.

The victory in the Mediterranean was announced on 11 September 1943, by the then Admiral Cunningham's message to the Admiralty, in terms traditional to the Royal Navy: 'Be pleased to inform their Lordships that the Italian battle fleet now lies at anchor under the guns of the fortress of Malta.'

An Italian submarine, which surrendered at Salerno, cruises past a British motor gunboat

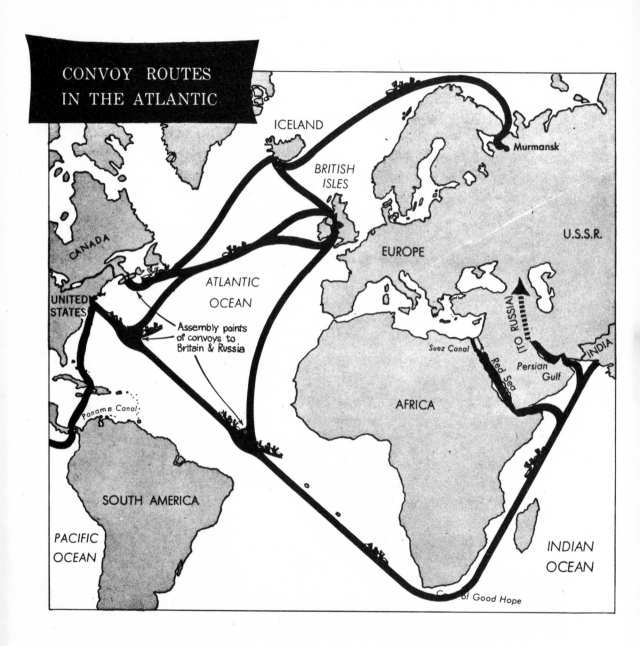

CONVOY ROUTES IN THE ATLANTIC

ICELAND

BRITISH ISLES

Murmansk

CANADA

EUROPE

U.S.S.R.

UNITED STATES

ATLANTIC OCEAN

Assembly points
of convoys to
Britain & Russia

(TO RUSSIA)

Suez Canal

Persian Gulf

INDIA

Panama Canal

AFRICA

SOUTH AMERICA

PACIFIC OCEAN

Red Sea

INDIAN OCEAN

Cape of Good Hope

32

Atlantic Naval Operations—1942-43

U-Boats off the American Coast

IN JANUARY 1942, only a few weeks after Germany declared war on the United States, German submarines arrived off the Atlantic coast of the United States to attack American coastal shipping. In the first four months of the year, German U-boats sank eighty-two

The American tanker R. P. Resor *in flames after being torpedoed by a German submarine off Manasquan, New Jersey*

EASTERN UNITED STATES

CANADA

MAINE

BOSTON

NEW YORK

WASHINGTON

ATLANTIC OCEAN

NEW ORLEANS

FLORIDA

GULF OF MEXICO

MIAMI

0 100 200 300
Scale of Miles

BAHAMAS

CUBA

DOMINICAN
REPUBLIC

MEXICO

CARIBBEAN SEA

JAMAICA

HAITI

PUERTO
RICO

⭐ AMERICAN BASES

merchant ships in the waters between northern Maine and southern Florida. Towering clouds of black smoke from burning merchant ships became a common sight along the coast. The beaches were covered with a scum of oil washed ashore from sunken tankers.

Although the United States Navy had a number of destroyers and other small escort vessels under construction, it simply did not have enough ships available at the beginning of 1942 to enable it to operate convoys along the coast. But Prime Minister Winston Churchill remembered the fifty destroyers Britain had received from America in 1940. In February 1942, he sent thirty-four small British escort warships to America. With their help the Americans were soon able to start a convoy system along the Atlantic coast. In May and June the Germans found that they were losing too many submarines to the American and British convoy escorts. They shifted their operations to the Gulf of Mexico and the Caribbean Sea, where the Americans still had too few escort ships to run convoys.

For several months the U-boats ranged over these waters almost unchecked. Again they sank large numbers of Allied merchant ships. By the autumn of 1942, however, the United States had enough new small warships to organize convoys along the southern coast of America, and Doenitz therefore recalled most of his wolf packs in order to make a new effort in the middle of the Atlantic.

Escape of the German Battle Cruisers

IN EARLY 1941, following their raids on Allied shipping in the North Atlantic, the German battle cruisers *Gneisenau* and *Scharnhorst*, and the cruiser *Prinz Eugen*, had taken refuge in the French sea-

35

A U.S. Navy Liberator bomber attacks a German U-boat in the South Atlantic

port of Brest. All three ships needed repairs, and all were damaged later in repeated raids on Brest. Nevertheless, by February 1942, they were again ready to go to sea.

Early on the night of 11 February, the three large ships slipped out of Brest and made a dash for Germany in a daring race through the English Channel. They were escorted by six destroyers, fifteen torpedo boats and twenty-four motor torpedo boats.

British naval forces in the Channel, under Sir Bertram Ramsay, had only six destroyers, six motor torpedo boats and six torpedo planes available. The Admiralty hoped that these, with the addition of planes of the R.A.F., would be able to prevent the German ships from escaping.

By chance, on the very night that the German ships started out from Brest, the radar sets broke down in both the R.A.F. planes patrolling the western part of the English Channel. Ramsay did not learn that the German ships were at sea until long after daylight on the foggy morning of 12 February. By this time, the German squadron was racing at full speed into the Strait of Dover.

The British torpedo planes, which had never worked together before, attacked at once, but all were shot down either by the strong *Luftwaffe* air escort, or by anti-aircraft fire from the ships. At the same time the British motor torpedo boats were being driven off by the German escort vessels.

By the time the German squadron reached the North Sea, a storm was raging. Though the six British destroyers and many R.A.F. planes now entered the fight, they had great difficulty in finding the German ships. They made a few attacks, but none were successful. It looked as though all the German ships would get away without suffering any damage. But as they were approaching the German coast, both battle cruisers struck British mines. The *Gneisenau* was slightly damaged. The *Scharnhorst*, which hit two mines, almost sank, but finally limped to Wilhelmshaven, where she was under repair for many months.

When the Germans attempted to seize the French fleet at Toulon in 1942, French sailors and officers scuttled their own ships

The Raid on Saint-Nazaire

DURING 1941-1942, tough British army commandos, working in close co-ordination with Royal Navy units, staged a number of raids against German installations along the French coast. The most thrilling of these adventurous attacks was made on the Atlantic coast seaport of Saint-Nazaire, in southern Brittany, on 27-28 March, 1942. Saint-Nazaire was an important U-boat base. It also had the only dry dock in Europe, outside Germany, that was large enough to handle the battleship *Tirpitz*. Fearful that the Germans might send the *Tirpitz* into the Atlantic on a raid like that of the *Bismarck,* and then base the great battleship at Saint-Nazaire, the British decided to destroy the dry dock. At the same time they intended to wreck the port facilities supporting German submarines.

The raiding naval force was under the command of R. E. D. Ryder; the commandos were led by A. C. Newman of the Essex Regiment. The principal aim of the plan was to run the old destroyer HMS *Campbeltown* into the lock gate on the dry dock, and then explode her. The *Campbeltown* was one of the fifty former American destroyers given to the British in exchange for military bases in 1940. For the Saint-Nazaire operation she was commanded by S. H. Beattie, and carried three tons of high explosives, timed to blow up two and a half hours after she rammed the lock gate.

The British raiding party approached the seaport secretly at night, but it was detected by the Germans only about a mile from the lock gate. When the shore defences opened up with intense fire, Beattie drove the old *Campbeltown* towards the lock gate at full speed. Just before his ship struck, Beattie fired two torpedoes into the gate. These had delayed-action fuses, set to go off at the same

39

A Nazi U-boat returns to its concrete garage at Lorient in France, after having sunk an American merchant ship. Installations such as this were one of the objectives of the Allied raid on Saint-Nazaire

time as the *Campbeltown's* explosive charge. As soon as the torpedoes were fired, the *Campbeltown* rammed her way more than thirty feet into the lock gate.

While the *Campbeltown* was attacking the dry dock, Newman and his commandos were dashing to the shore in motor-boats, despite a hail of fire from the German defenders. For several hours Saint-Nazaire was in an uproar of confused fighting. The Germans sank eighteen of the British motor-boats. The remaining seven, severely damaged and loaded to overflowing with wounded men, pulled away from the seaport shortly before dawn. Most of the remaining commandos were killed or captured, though a few escaped inland and later managed to get back to England. Four of the seven remaining motor-boats were rescued by British destroyers waiting offshore. The other three returned to England under their own power, shooting down a *Luftwaffe* bomber during the rough, exciting trip.

The few survivors of the raid were discouraged. They thought they had failed, since the time fuses in the torpedoes and in the *Campbeltown* had not gone off. The next morning a number of German senior officers went on board the *Campbeltown* and began to work out how to remove her and repair the lock gate. Suddenly the ship exploded, killing almost everybody on board. Then, as the Germans tried to rescue those who had survived the blast, the two torpedoes in the lock gate exploded, killing most of those left in the vicinity. The lock gate and the dry dock were completely destroyed. The raid had been a complete success after all.

A Change in the German Naval Command

IN THE AUTUMN OF 1942, the Allies resumed their convoys to Murmansk. German submarines and aircraft again took severe toll of British ships, but increased numbers of escorts, particularly the new escort carriers, made it possible for most of the supply ships to get through to northern Russia.

In January 1943, the German pocket battleship *Lutzow* and the cruiser *Hipper*, accompanied by several destroyers, attacked a convoy in the desolate waters between North Cape and Bear Island. After a sharp fight, the Allied escort ships repulsed the attack. When Hitler heard the news he flew into a rage against

Grand Admiral Erich Raeder, commander of the German navy, and accused him of not operating the navy properly. Raeder resigned, and Hitler put Doenitz in charge of the German navy. For most of the rest of 1943 Doenitz, the submarine expert, kept all the German surface ships in port and relied entirely upon his U-boats.

The Battle of the Atlantic Reaches a Crisis

DOENITZ WAS NOT entirely satisfied with the results of his submarine offensive in 1942. The Allies had lost some 1,700 ships, a total of over 8,000,000 tons, and the U-boats had accounted for more than three-quarters of this total. But in that same year the Allies had built some 7,000,000 tons of shipping. For the first time in the war, new Allied ships were being produced almost as fast as the Germans could sink them.

Doenitz, however, thought that in 1943 his submarines could sink many more ships than the Allies would be able to build. In 1942, he had started out with only ninety-one U-boats operational. In January of 1943, he had more than 200. He ordered an all-out attack on Allied shipping.

Despite bad weather, the U-boats sank 359,000 tons of Allied shipping in February, and 627,000 tons in March. In that month the German wolf packs fought a fierce battle against one large Allied convoy, in which they sank twenty-one ships. They lost only one submarine.

It turned out, however, that this was the last big U-boat victory. In April and May several new escort carriers arrived to join the Allied convoys, followed later in the year by the first of

42

The tanker Rapana, *a merchant aircraft carrier*

the new 'merchant aircraft carriers'. The latter were all tankers
or grain ships, because these types of merchantmen took on their
cargoes through pipes—which would not prevent a flight deck
being fitted—whereas solid cargo has to be lowered through
open hatches.

Long-range American bombers began to appear in great numbers over the central Atlantic, where the U-boats had operated
so successfully in the previous two years. In May, the U-boats and
Allied convoys fought a series of battles that showed how the tide
had turned.

In early May a pack of twelve submarines found a convoy that
had been scattered in a storm. In two days these U-boats sank
nine ships. Then the escorts began to strike back. In the next few
days they sank eleven of the attackers without losing a single ship.
A few days later, another Allied convoy lost five ships and sank five
submarines. Near the end of the month, the escorts of a third
convoy sank six submarines without losing a ship.

May 1943 was the turning point in the Battle of the Atlantic.

In that month the submarines sank 165,000 tons of Allied shipping. At the same time the Allies sank 40 U-boats. The story was the same throughout the rest of 1943. Only 3,600,000 tons of Allied shipping were sunk during that year, and Doenitz lost 237 of his submarines. Even more important, Allied shipyards produced the amazing total of 14,500,000 tons of merchant shipping. By the end of the year, this tremendous spurt in construction had more than replaced all the shipping losses the Allies had suffered during the first four years of the war.

The Tirpitz *Threat*

ALTHOUGH DOENITZ did not use his surface ships in 1943, the British continued to worry about the presence of the powerful *Tirpitz* in the German anchorage at Alta Fjord, in the most northerly part of Norway.

Alta Fjord was beyond the range of British bombers based in Scotland, but the Germans knew that British carrier planes could attack the *Tirpitz* in her anchorage. They had moored her close to shore and camouflaged her cleverly, in order to confuse attacking airmen. On the land-side, towering cliffs protected the great battleship, making it difficult for British planes to make low-level bombing or torpedo attacks. On the water-side, the Germans had completely enclosed the ship in a steel-mesh torpedo net. No surface vessel or submarine could approach her without going through minefields and passing for miles within range of powerful coastal defence guns lining both sides of the long, winding channel of Alta Fjord.

The British tried a number of times to attack the *Tirpitz* from

Allied Shipping Losses and Shipping Construction

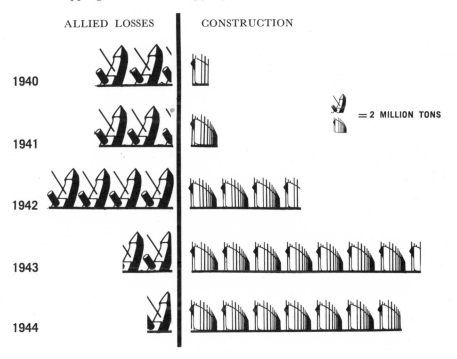

ALLIED LOSSES   CONSTRUCTION

1940

1941

1942

1943

1944

= 2 MILLION TONS

Speed in Sea Warfare

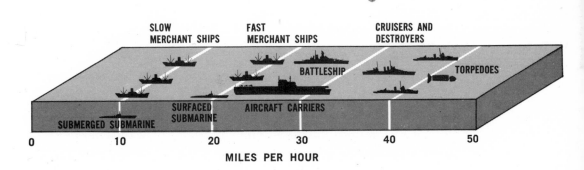

SLOW MERCHANT SHIPS

FAST MERCHANT SHIPS

CRUISERS AND DESTROYERS

BATTLESHIP

TORPEDOES

SUBMERGED SUBMARINE

SURFACED SUBMARINE

AIRCRAFT CARRIERS

0   10   20   30   40   50

MILES PER HOUR

the air, and failed. Then they decided to try midget submarines. Three of these little vessels, each manned by four men, stealthily crept up the fjord late in the evening of 21 September, 1943. Each boat carried a powerful charge of explosive weighing two tons. Shortly after midnight they approached the battleship.

One of the three midgets was detected and sunk by the Germans. The other two succeeded in working their way past the torpedo net, and placed their charges on the bottom of the fjord, directly under the *Tirpitz*. A few minutes later, time fuses set off the charges. A terrific explosion raised the huge battleship several feet in the water, ripping holes in her bottom. Her engines, rudders, propellers and gun-control equipment were all seriously damaged. Because of her remarkable construction, the *Tirpitz* did not sink, but the Germans realized that it would take six months or a year to make her seaworthy again. Both the attacking submarines were sunk, but six of their crew survived, only to be captured by the Germans.

The Triumph of Allied Sea Power

The Last Cruise of the Scharnhorst

LATE IN 1943, because he was disappointed by the failure of his submarine offensive, Doenitz decided to use surface ships in renewed attacks against the Murmansk convoys. At that time the only large German ship available was the battle cruiser *Scharnhorst*, at Alta Fjord in northern Norway.

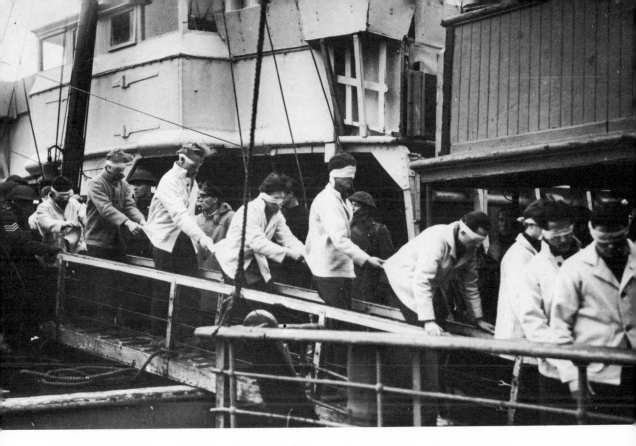

Blindfolded survivors of the Scharnhorst *land at a British port on their way to internment*

Towards the end of December, a large Allied convoy was heading for Murmansk, escorted by nearly twenty destroyers. Near by was a covering force of three British cruisers and four destroyers under the command of Robert Burnett. East of Iceland were cruising the battleship HMS *Duke of York*, a cruiser, and four destroyers, under Bruce Fraser.

German planes and submarines discovered the convoy in the area between North Cape and Bear Island. Doenitz immediately ordered Erich Bey to attack the convoy with the *Scharnhorst*. On Christmas Eve the battle cruiser sailed out from Alta Fjord, accompanied by five destroyers. A storm was raging in the Arctic Ocean; tremendous waves tossed the German destroyers wildly. Bey sent a radio message to German naval headquarters, asking if he should continue. Doenitz ordered him to carry on with the attack against the Allied convoy.

The British intercepted these radio messages, and so learned that the *Scharnhorst* was at sea. The convoy turned north, past Bear Island, while Burnett's cruiser squadron raced to intercept the German battle cruiser. At the same time, Fraser's squadron steamed eastwards as rapidly as possible to join the action.

At about 9.15 in the morning of 26 December, the *Scharnhorst* approached the area where Bey expected to find the convoy. Suddenly the mid-winter Arctic darkness was lit up by an illuminating star-shell bursting over the German ship. Instead of meeting the convoy, Bey unexpectedly found himself engaged with Burnett's three cruisers which had been secretly stalking the *Scharnhorst* for nearly an hour. Turning southwards, Bey pulled away from the British cruisers, then swung westwards again to try to find the convoy.

Burnett positioned his cruisers across the front of the convoy. Shortly after noon the German battle cruiser approached the convoy and the British cruisers opened fire. The *Scharnhorst* turned and fled to the south-eastward.

Burnett came in from the west, heading to cross the *Scharnhorst's* bows, and at 4.48 in the afternoon the *Duke of York* illuminated the enemy with star-shell. At 12,000 yards the 14-inch guns of the *Duke of York* opened fire. Their shells smashed into the surprised German ship. Turning sharply north-eastwards, the *Scharnhorst* sped away from her pursuers. The fast German battle cruiser had pulled almost out of range when one 14-inch shell from the *Duke*

HMS Duke of York

of York struck her after part, thus slowing her down considerably.

Now the British destroyers closed in to fire their torpedoes. Despite heavy fire from the *Scharnhorst,* they scored four hits. The German ship was almost stopped in the water. Shells from the *Duke of York* and the British cruisers set her on fire. The cruisers and destroyers then hit her with seven more torpedoes. At 7.45, in a cloud of smoke, the big German vessel sank. For an hour the British destroyers searched for survivors through the stormy darkness, but they could rescue only thirty-six men out of the 1,900 that had comprised the German crew.

49

The Invasion Armada

THE GREAT ALLIED amphibious invasions of World War II began in October 1942, with Operation TORCH, which wrested French North Africa from the, pro-German, Vichy French. This was followed by the Allied invasions of Sicily and south Italy in July and September 1943, and the landing at Anzio in January 1944. Each of these had been large, complex operations, involving the closest teamwork between the two great Allied navies, and between British and American soldiers and sailors. But these had been merely preparation for the mammoth amphibious assault that was planned for the invasion of France in early June 1944.

This invasion was known as Operation OVERLORD. The more than 2,000,000 Allied soldiers, sailors and airmen who were involved in this gigantic effort were under the command of the American General Dwight D. Eisenhower. The naval commander responsible for getting the soldiers to the beaches, and then for giving them gunfire support to keep them ashore, was the British Admiral Sir Bertram H. Ramsay. Under his immediate control were 5,000 British, American and Free French vessels of all types: warships, troop transports, landing ships, supply vessels.

The landings were originally planned for 5 June, but bad weather delayed them for one day. When the leading troops finally hit the Normandy beaches just after dawn on 6 June, Ramsay had over eighty warships pounding the German shore defences. These included six battleships, fifteen cruisers, and some sixty destroyers and destroyer escorts.

D-Day : barrage balloons hover over Omaha Beach before breakwaters and piers are set up

The land fighting was bitter and intense on that grim day. The main reason for the success of the Allied landings was, of course, the courage and determination of the soldiers. But the soldiers could never have overcome the shore defences nor have driven off the German counter-attacks if it had not been for the accurate and heavy fire delivered by the Allied warships, and the splendid support given by R.A.F. and U.S. Air Force planes based in southern England. It was a victory in which soldier, sailor and airman alike could take pride. But above all it was a victory for sea power possible only because the Allied navies—and particularly the Royal Navy—had established superiority over the Axis fleets in the previous five long years of war.

D-Day: L.C.T.s ready to set off across the Channel

The Last Days of Hitler's Navy

The End of the Tirpitz

AFTER THE SINKING of the *Scharnhorst,* the Germans were able to do little more damage to the well-protected Murmansk convoys. U-boats and bombers sank a few supply ships, but each time the attackers lost heavily. Meanwhile, in northern Norway, the Germans were hard at work repairing the damaged *Tirpitz,* and by April 1944 the great ship was almost ready for action.

Remembering the damage caused by the *Tirpitz's* sister ship, the *Bismarck,* the British decided to make a supreme effort to destroy the *Tirpitz* before she got out. Before dawn on 3 April, a force of five British carriers secretly approached the northern Norwegian coast. As day broke the first wave of British carrier planes swept down over Alta Fjord and dropped several bombs squarely on the *Tirpitz.* They lost only one plane to the surprised Germans. A few minutes later the second wave closed in. It scored several more hits, and one more plane was lost. Fifteen 1,000-pound bombs had hit the *Tirpitz.* Nearly 300 of the ship's crew had been killed, and guns and radar equipment had been severely damaged. But not a single bomb had penetrated the ship's armoured deck made of 8-inch steel.

Although the British attempted further attacks on the *Tirpitz* while she was again being repaired in Alta Fjord, they were for a long time unable to repeat the success of their April attack. Then, on 15 September, a long-range British bomber again damaged the battleship, this time with a 6,000-pound bomb. The *Tirpitz* sailed for Tromsoe, where there were better repair facilities and better anti-aircraft defences.

In October and November the British bombers renewed their attacks on the *Tirpitz*, this time with great 'blockbuster', six-ton

The sunken Tirpitz *lies just off the coast in Tromsoe Fjord*

bombs. Finally, on 12 November, the indomitable ship was hit by several of these blockbusters and sank, carrying with her 1,200 of her crew. The British could now be sure there would be no more raids like those of the *Bismarck*.

Doenitz Tries Again

DOENITZ KNEW that he had suffered a disastrous defeat in the Battle of the Atlantic in 1943, but he believed that he could reverse the tide in 1944. He was a practical, hard-headed sailor who had carefully studied the lessons of his earlier defeat. One fact stood out with particular clarity: Allied escort ships and planes had been sinking many of his submarines just after they had fired their torpedoes.

At that time, a submarine had to be near the surface when it fired its torpedoes so that it could see the target through its periscope. The periscope protruded above the water, and could be spotted by the enemy. The torpedo, too, clearly indicated its own presence as soon as it was fired. On its way to the target it stirred up a wake, or path in the water, just like that of a small boat. From its wake, the Allied escort ships were able to estimate the torpedo's starting point. They would then drop heavy explosive, or depth charges, on that spot and rip the submarine apart. Although a submarine could dive rapidly following an attack, its weak underwater electric engines could not move it fast enough to get it out of range of the Allied escorts. Furthermore, the escorts were equipped with underwater listening devices, known as 'sonar' and 'asdic', which could pick up the sound of the submarine's engines and indicate where the depth charges should be dropped.

Doenitz decided to find some way to sink Allied ships without using torpedoes. He believed that his U-boats could sink just as many merchant ships—possibly more—if they laid great quantities of mines along the approaches to Allied seaports. They could drop the mines, and then get away when no Allied warships were around to attack them.

This plan, however, did not work out in the way that Doenitz had expected. The Allies had built many minesweepers, and they regularly swept all the shipping channels leading to Allied seaports. The Germans sank very few ships by this U-boat mining campaign.

Doenitz then tried a new kind of 'homing' torpedo that could be fired at the convoys from a great distance, so that the U-boats could dive and hide deep under the water again before the Allied escorts could reach them. The new weapons were called 'acoustic' torpedoes, because they could be attracted by the sound of a ship's propellers in the water. Every time an acoustic torpedo came at all near to a ship, it would turn and 'home' straight for the propellers.

The new torpedoes were very successful, but only for a short time. The Allies soon understood what was happening, and built noise-making gadgets known as 'foxers'. These were towed behind the ships and made more noise than ship's propellers. The acoustic torpedoes homed on the foxers and exploded harmlessly in the water behind the ships.

Doenitz knew that another important reason for the Allied successes in 1943 was their increased use of aircraft—including the fighters on the escort carriers, and the long-range, shore-based patrol planes. He therefore put more anti-aircraft guns on his U-boats and ordered them to fight it out with Allied planes whenever these planes attacked them on the surface. But this plan, too, failed to work out as well as he had expected. The U-boats shot down a few Allied planes, but the submarines had no protection against powerful aircraft rockets. In these air-against-surface duels, the submarines usually lost.

A New German Submarine

THOUGH HE WAS DISAPPOINTED by the failure of his new methods of attack on Allied shipping, Doenitz had yet another trick up his sleeve. German scientists had discovered ways of keeping submarines almost constantly under the water, so that they could not be seen by aircraft or detected by the radar sets of Allied surface escorts.

Up to this time, submarines were not able to use diesel or petrol engines under the water because they burned up the submarine's oxygen supply and spread poisonous fumes inside the vessel. Submarines' underwater engines were electric, run from large storage batteries, which had to be frequently recharged. In order to recharge the batteries, it was necessary to surface the submarine and run the diesel engines. Even though this was usually done at night, the surfaced submarines were often found by the radar sets of Allied warships and planes, and were then attacked. Many of the U-boats had been sunk in this way.

In 1944, the Germans introduced a new and simple way for a U-boat to use its diesel engines while running submerged. A device called a *schnorkel* was added to the submarine. The *schnorkel* was a long, telescoping tube-within-a-tube. The inner, air-intake tube extended a few feet above the water and was equipped with a valve which closed automatically if the *schnorkel* accidentally went under the water. Through the outer, or exhaust tube, the poisonous diesel fumes were blown out of the submarine. With this device, the submarine could stay submerged several feet below the surface of the water, with only the tip of its *schnorkel* sticking out. This was too small to show up on a radar screen, and it could not be seen from surface ships unless they were right beside it.

Submarines fitted with *schnorkels* rarely had to come to the surface, and could move so rapidly under the water that they were able to get away from most escort ships. Because of this, they were much more effective than the earlier U-boats had been. But by this time there were so many Allied escort ships, and these had such excellent underwater weapons of attack, that the new *schnorkel* submarines had a hard time finding an opportunity to fire their torpedoes without being attacked at once. As soon as a torpedo was fired, escort aircraft converged on the spot, and they could usually see from the air the outline of the submarine below the surface of the water. Despite the *schnorkel*, the Allies continued to gain in the Battle of the Atlantic.

By 1945 German scientists had designed newer, bigger and faster U-boats with an entirely new, silent kind of engine. Doenitz hoped these would be more successful than the *schnorkel* submarines, but he never had a chance to find out. In May, just as the first new submarine was getting ready to go to sea, the Allied armies overran Germany.

The German Navy Disappears

In 1944 and 1945 the Germans made few attempts to operate surface ships in either the Atlantic Ocean or the North Sea. German warships were still busy, however, in the Baltic. They

A German U-boat surrenders on the high seas to an American task force

protected iron-ore convoys against Russian submarines, and acted as escorts for troop and supply convoys. This was particularly important after the German armies in the Baltic States were cut off by Russian victories in late 1944. The pocket battleships *Scheer* and *Lutzow,* in combination with cruisers and destroyers, did much useful work escorting convoys and preventing Russian surface ships from gaining control of the Baltic.

During these last months of the war, the few remaining German surface warships disappeared one by one. Some were sunk by Allied bombers, some blown up by mines laid by Allied aircraft. Early in 1945 the *Gneisenau,* being repaired at Gdynia, was scuttled by her crew to prevent her being captured by the advancing Russian army. In April, Allied air raids destroyed most of the remaining surface vessels of the German navy. When the war ended, only two cruisers and a few destroyers were left to surrender to the Allies, together with 400 submarines.

The German navy had kept up the struggle to the very end with all its dwindling strength and ability. German sailors had fought hard. German scientists had shown great ingenuity in inventing new weapons and in improving the fighting qualities of German ships and U-boats. But the cause for which these men fought had been unworthy. Their leader, Hitler, had been an evil man whose ambitions finally ruined his country. Furthermore, the Germans had been opposed by equal courage, skill, determination and scientific ingenuity on the part of the navies of the two great Western Allies which, together with Russia, though unprepared for war, finally marshalled their overwhelming power to crush Hitler. But this could never have brought Germany to its knees had it not been for the wise *use* of sea power by the leaders of Britain and America.

Index